THE BRANCH LINE AGE
the minor railways of the British Isles
in memorium and retrospect

Branch line exploration in Scotland sees a J36 class 0-6-0 drifting slowly into Lennoxtown en route to Aberfoyle, a popular resort in the Trossachs. Passenger trains were rare on this lengthy line, and this was the first special train to run after a ban of six years over closed lines in Scotland. The line was opened on 5 November 1866 as the Blane Valley Railway to Dumgoyne. Lennoxtown had two stations just a few yards apart, one being the original terminus of the Edinburgh and Glasgow Railway, which was opened on 5 July 1858. The line shown was closed to passengers in September 1951, seven years before this photograph was taken.

The highly spruced-up locomotive is a North British 0-6-0 class J36 (LNER classification), and is of a class that dated from the 1880s. A feature of Scottish locomotive sheds was to paint up the front number-plate with a coloured background; this locomotive carries an Eastfield plate and duty number 189. The stock appears to be entirely Gresley bow-enders, some of which were running until a year or so ago. On occasions such as this, where a train had not been seen for several years, local people would emerge goggle-eyed from nearby housing estates to witness what would be on many occasions the last passenger train to traverse their local line.

The Branch Line Age

the minor railways of the British Isles in memoriam
and retrospect

C. J. Gammell

MOORLAND PUBLISHING COMPANY

ISBN 0 903485 38 9

© C. J. Gammell 1976

Printed in Great Britain by
Wood Mitchell & Co Ltd, Stoke on Trent

For the Publishers
Moorland Publishing Company
The Market Place, Hartington,
Buxton, Derbys, SK17 0AL

Contents

Preface

A sad sight in the countryside today is the decline of the railway. Closed stations, uprooted sidings, singled lines, stations that were main line junctions reduced to unstaffed halts and abandoned branch lines. What were branch lines like?

In the heyday of railways the maps of the British Isles showed an intricate and complex web of minor railways radiating out from numerous trunk lines. No town or village of any importance was without a railway. Some towns had even more than one line. During the days prior to the 1923 grouping routes duplicated one another over long distances, such was the intense competition between rival companies. Each railway company had its own distinctive style. Signals, buildings, platform furniture, fences as well as locomotives and rolling stock, all had the imprint of the owning company. The differences even persisted after nationalisation and can be seen on some buildings to this day.

All minor railways conveyed their passengers with a puposefulness and leisure that belonged to the nineteenth century – the age of the horse, the years before the all too common motor vehicle would infiltrate into every country lane and village.

To arrive at the station, having covered a considerable distance during the day, and be met or greeted by friends waiting, was a formality for the passenger and his host. To alight and walk down the long winding station road to the village, or to cross muddy fields along uneven footpaths was a way to make a visit which had made travelling an event to be remembered. The traveller had accomplished his journey and arrived.

An ex-Great Southern & Western Railway 0-6-0, class 101 No 133, dating from the last century, pauses at Loo Bridge on the Kenmore branch County Kerry, Eire, in 1958.

Southern Region

1   The branch line scene as viewed from the other side of the fence by a passing motorist at High Halden Road, an intermediate station on the former Kent and East Sussex Railway, in August 1952. The superb two-way signal with lower spectacle and lamp was a feature here, although few passengers and even fewer trains seem to be in evidence. The section of the K & ESR from Robertsbridge to Rolvenden (then called Tenterden) was opened as the Rother Valley Railway in 1900 and to Tenterden Town in 1903, the original Tenterden station then being renamed Rolvenden. High Halden Road was on the northerly extension from Tenterden to Headcorn which opened in 1905, when the railway changed its name to Kent and East Sussex.

The K & ESR was engineered by Mr (later Lt-Col) H.F. Stephens and subsequently managed by him for more than 30 years. A feature of Colonel Stephen's group of railways was that nothing was ever thrown away and old locomotives and carriages would moulder unused in sidings for years, eventually becoming engulfed in weeds. He refused to merge any of his lines at the grouping in 1923, although having every opportunity to do so. Hence the K & ESR remained independent until absorbed into the Southern Region of British Railways on Nationalisation in 1948. The line was closed to passengers throughout on 2 January 1954. The line north of Tenterden was closed completely on this date, but the original Rother Valley section, from Robertsbridge to Tenterden remained open for goods until June 1961. It is intended to reopen the 10 miles between Tenterden and Bodiam in stages; the first 2½ miles from Tenterden to beyond Rolvenden is already in operation. (*J.H. Aston*).

2 Tenterden Town with an A1X
class locomotive and a rather short
train from Robertsbridge, shortly
before closure to passengers in 1954.
This famous engine (BR No 32655)
is now preserved in its original
London, Brighton and South Coast
Railway livery of bright yellow as
LB & SCR No 55 *Stepney*, on the
Bluebell Railway – a preserved
section of the former LB & SCR line
between Lewes and East Grinstead.
The yellow livery was introduced by
its designer, William Stroudley, as
'improved engine green', supposedly
to get round the prejudices of the
LB & SCR management and staff to
any locomotive colour but green.
Two other A1X class locomotives
(popularly known as 'Terriers') are
now preserved at Rolvenden on the
K & ESR, they are ex-BR(SR) Nos
32650 and 32670, now known as No
10 *Sutton* (see Fig 17) and No 3
Bodiam, respectively. The latter is
the only original K & ESR locomotive surviving, having been built
in 1872 as LB & SCR *Poplar* and
purchased by the K & ESR in 1901,
surviving to be absorbed into
BR(SR) at Nationalisation.

3 A break for the train crew at Allhallows in July 1955. This line was opened by the Southern Railway in the nineteen thirties as part of a land speculation and development deal of which the SR was very fond. The expected commuters did not materialise and as a result the line declined. The station nameboard is of the standard type of that period with letters mounted behind a glass panel and the astute observer will notice these still in use on the region today. The locomotive is an H class 0-4-4T on the train for Gravesend. The stock shown here is London, Brighton and South Coast Railway pattern. This two coach push and pull set, with long commode handles by the doors, had a corridor running down the side of the interior of the coach, the compartments not having doors. This line finally expired in December 1961, but the portion from Hoo Junction to Grain still prospers with oil refinery traffic. (*J.H. Aston*).

4 Beluncle, on the Isle of Grain branch (or Hundred of Hoo as the working timetable showed it) in the 1930s was a typical Southern Railway branch line. The South-Eastern and Chatham Railway management committee notice seems to have a white coat of paint with black lettering; these notices can still be seen at a few locations on the former system. The bridge restriction plates are also probably SE & CR. The line closed to passengers in December 1961.

5   Brasted Station on the Westerham branch, which in the final years of the line's history became an unstaffed halt. Locomotive No 31500 arrives with the 4.50 pm from Dunton Green on 14 May 1960. South Eastern Railway architecture is very much in evidence in this picture, from the slate over-roof to the wood weatherboarding and looped railings supported on rounded-off old rails. The SE & CR lamp standards with barley-stick stems were easily distinguishable and varied from their London and Southern Western Railway counterparts which had less twist. Here, another H class 0-4-4T of Tonbridge shed arrives with a push and pull of LB & SCR stock. Because the SR in pre-war years concentrated on electrification much pre-group stock survived into BR days. (*J.H. Aston*).

6   The same location two years later looking towards Westerham shows the vegetation slowly taking over as the rails disappear.

7 The death of an English branch line, the last day on the Westerham branch, 28 October 1961. A well known resort for London-based branch line visitors, the Westerham line managed to maintain its pre-group appearance. This line was the subject of an abortive preservation attempt. After many years of negotiation the scheme fell through, and all prospects were eliminated by the construction of the Sevenoaks by-pass. The line would have made an ideal preservation project as the largest locomotives could be accommodated. Here is locomotive duty No 239 of Tonbridge with H class No 31518. (*J. A. V. Smallwood*)

8 South-Eastern memorablia at Dunton Green; regional colours of the station nameplates intermingle with one-mantle Suggs patent gas-lighting. The lamps, when ignited by a porter carrying a long pole with a hook on the end, gave a distinctive 'pop', followed by a low continuous burping sound. (*J. A. V. Smallwood*)

Three views of one station from heyday to closure. The Elham Valley Railway was never a financial success, as it was constructed solely to keep the London, Chatham and Dover Railway out of Folkestone. It was a relic of the days of severe competition and duplication of routes between the SER and the LC & DR prior to their amalgamation in 1899. Until that date the railways of Kent virtually consisted of these two companies. Lyminge, on the Elham Valley was probably the biggest settlement that the line passed through.

9   Of interest in this pre-war picture, is the slotted signal mounted on the goods dock. The station roof is typical SE & CR in style with curved corrugated iron and dog-tooth finish. The lamps are oil, and are inserted in their holders. The stock consists of a short wheel-base ex-works vehicle, followed by a birdcage set. The H class 0-4-4T appears to be in SR green livery.

10   The second view shows a summer scene from a different angle probably taken shortly before closure. Note the SE & CR shunt signal on the cattle dock, also the portable fencing. In this picture the 'gents' sign is of standard SE & CR enamel finish, some examples of these are still to be found on the Southern region to this day.

11   Scene three shows the aftermath, the station house has been sold off and is in use a private dwelling. This scene today has been completely erased. although incredibly enough two stations on this line remain intact as private houses. Passenger services were finally withdrawn in 1947, and this picture was taken shortly afterwards.

12   Seen in the goods yard at Partridge Green in the winter of 1959, a delightful specimen of a London, Brighton and South Coast Railway oil lamp. The lamp seems to have fallen into disuse, but is probably original and dating from the line's construction in the last century. The use to which it had been put to originally has long since been forgotten.

13   Christ's Hospital in Sussex sees
the arrival of an Ivatt class 2MT
2-6-2T locomotive and three-coach
set from Horsham. The railman is
holding the train staff to give to the
fireman as the train enters the single-
line section to run to Guildford. The
guard keeps a sharp eye on
proceedings from the rear. The
Guildford-Horsham line was swept
away at the height of the Beeching
purges and the line closed to all
traffic two days after this picture was
taken. Christ's Hospital was opened
in 1902 to serve the nearby school of
that name which had just moved
from London. Up until its closure in
1965 the station had a distinct
Edwardian air about it, the solid
wooden panelling being typical of
the LB & SCR style.

14   The first station down the line
from Christ's Hospital was at
Slinfold, a little way from the village
and one of the remotest stations on
the line. The impressive station
buildings belie the lack of amenity;
many station houses had no
electricity, no gas and sometimes no
running water. When the line was
opened in 1865 an entrepreneur built
a hotel at Slinfold, but needless to
say the expected custom did not
materialize and the hotel was sold off
and became a private house.

15 Rudgwick, on the same line as Slinfold in the final days of the line's existence in June 1965. When the line closed it had not quite made its centenary. In this picture most of the traffic has gone, the goods yard has been closed as also has the signal box. The arms have been removed from the signalpost and the station staff disbanded. 41299 pauses for a time before proceeding to Horsham with a near-empty train. A fine example of a LB & SCR country station with one or two post-grouping embellishments.

16 Baynards was one of the most colourful stations on the Southern Region and won many prizes in the station gardens competitions. The speciality of the station was dahlia planting, the beds of which can be seen behind the starting signal. Baynards was another of those stations that were built to serve a nearby house – in this case Baynards Park, a Tudor mansion. Note the all-wooden signal box and point rodding that runs under the footway.

17 The Hayling Island branch was a remarkable survival with locomotives dating from the 1870s. The A1X class of course needs no introduction to railway enthusiasts and here No 32650 is seen running bunker first at Langstone in October 1963, one month before the line closed. The fireman has been caught pushing the coals down the bunker, which, as the locomotive once worked on the Isle of Wight, has been lowered. Note the open ground-frame by the crossing keeper's hut. This locomotive is now preserved at Rolvenden on the Kent and East Sussex Railway as No 10 *Sutton*.

15

18 Mayfield, on the Eastbourne to Tunbridge Wells line with standard class 4 tank locomotive 80142 arriving. This picture was taken shortly before closure in June 1965. The lack of custom is another noticeable feature here. Looking at the huge empty station one can just imagine the large crowds that once thronged these platforms in the 1890s. This station had a subway, the LB & SCR favouring them to footbridges, even in the most rural areas. This line was opened in 1880 and formed the shortest route from London to Eastbourne, being $4\frac{1}{2}$ miles shorter than the route via Lewes.

19   Ashey, on the Isle of Wight
Central line to Newport with an 02
class 0-4-4T leaving in June 1960
with a through-train to Cowes. The
stock is a mixed bag of SE & CR
and LB & SCR vehicles; the SE &
CR coaches still had family saloons
in them, an Edwardian practice, as
large families were the norm in that
period so the companies provided
accommodation in large saloons
seating 10 to 15 persons. The line to
Newport closed in 1966, when steam
also finally finished in the island. A
feature of Isle of Wight trains was
that they were air braked, unlike the
rest of the region's steam trains. Part
of this line is now preserved.

20 The South Western scene, an M7 class 0-4-4T arriving at Alresford in the early fifties. This line from Alton to Winchester was closed as recently as 5 February 1973. In this scene the only evidence of group ownership is the Southern Railway notice board. The M7 class Drummond tank engines lasted well into the 1960s and were a feature of London and South Western Railway branch lines. This one is push and pull fitted with L & SWR stock. The signals are of interest being L & SWR lower quadrants, but the interesting one here is the L & SWR shunt-ahead signal enabling the driver to take his train past the stop signal to make a shunt. This branch line was nicknamed the 'Watercress Line' as Alresford has been the main source of watercress in Southern England for about a century. Most of this was transported by rail from Alresford station until September 1963, when it was transferred to road. Alresford is now the head-quarters of the Mid-Hants Railway Preservation Society, whose parent company, Winchester and Alton Railway Limited, attempted to save the whole of this branch with an unsuccessful public share issue in June 1975. A less ambitious scheme to reopen the line north of Alresford at least as far as Ropley was the subject of a second, successful, share issue in December 1975.

21 Privett on the one time Meon Valley Railway, which was built by the London and South Western Railway as an alternative route to Portsmouth. The L & SWR were determined to keep the Great Western Railway out of the Solent area and so this line was built to main line standards. This picture, taken in the early fifties, again shows an M7 class No 54 on a Fareham to Alton stopping train. The pre-war lettering is showing through the paintwork on the locomotive cab side. Notice the whitewashed colonnade – a relic of wartime when lighting was restricted. The glass roof on the building has been painted over – another wartime practice (most stations still have their roofs painted over to this day). This line did not even last to see the Beeching purges, having succumbed on 7 February 1955. (E. C. Griffith)

Western Region

22   Edington Burtle, on the Somerset and Dorset Joint Railway, in 1964. This station was once the junction of the Bridgewater branch with the original line of the Somerset Central Railway from Glastonbury to Highbridge and Burnham-on-Sea. The Somerset Central Railway was opened in 1854 as a broad-gauge line worked by the Bristol and Exeter Railway Company, but became standard gauge on amalgamation with the Dorset Central Railway in 1862 to give a through route from the Bristol Channel at Burnham to the English Channel at Poole. The line was transferred to BR Western Region from Southern Region in 1958, after being operated jointly by the Midland Railway and the London and South Western Railway, and subsequently their successors the LMS and SR from 1875 to Nationalisation. It retained unique operating procedures and train headcodes, giving it a strong independent spirit until closure in March 1966. In this view a wheezy GWR 0-6-0 pauses en route to Evercreech Junction, evidence of the Westernisation that took place after 1958.

23   Pylle, on the same line with a class 2 tank approaching in February 1964. The way in which the station has been run down and shows signs of decline is evident. The station has been unstaffed and has been renamed Pylle (Halt), the signalbox has been closed and the passing loop taken out (as long ago as 1929), but the buildings remain sound and in good order. This is a good example of a well constructed station and adjacent house, all in local stone, which gives an idea of the completeness of some of the more rural stations.

24 Abbotsbury, on the short branch from Upwey near Weymouth on the GWR – a branch line in the heyday of railways as seen through the eyes of a Dorset cameraman. This Edwardian scene, with the inhabitants turned out in their Sunday best, shows how tidy and well kept the station was. A chocolate and cream push and pull auto-trailer car simmers in the platform while the crew join in the group. This picture is quite a contrast with some of the views of branches in decline. The local stone finish gives a good idea of the style of small GWR buildings.

The Great Western Railway introduced steam railmotors in 1903, being a coach with an integral vertically-boilered steam locomotive at one end, driving directly onto one of the supporting bogies. But, proving slow and underpowered, they were all withdrawn by 1910 and most of the carriage portions were converted into auto-trailer cars. These worked with special auto-fitted locomotives, which enabled the driver to work the train from the front compartment of the coach when the locomotive was pushing at the rear, the fireman remaining on the locomotive. Hence the train could work in either direction without any need for the engine to run round its train at the end of the journey.

25 Helston in the fifties, showing the cramped layout of the single-platform station. GWR platform-trolleys and parcels seem to take up most of the room, leaving little space for passengers. The branch was opened in 1887 and was worked by the GWR, the Helston Railway Company being absorbed by the GWR in 1898. The line was 8¾ miles long and single track and, surprisingly, built as standard gauge in an area which remained broad gauge until 1892. Helston was famous for the first bus service operated by the GWR in 1903 to the Lizard. The line closed to passengers on 5 November 1962.

26 14XX class No 1450 0-4-2T jogs out of Tiverton Junction on 23 August 1964 with brakevans for the Hemyock milk traffic, which alas is no more. The twisting Culm Valley Light Railway was opened on 29 May 1876 as an independent company, but was taken over by the GWR. The line was well known for the slowness of the trains, which, when composed of mixed passenger and goods traffic, waited about at the intermediate stations of Culmstock and Uffculme while the 0-4-2T performed some leisurely shunting.

27 Two views of the Culm Valley Railway, as the Hemyock branch was known. This delightful GWR branch (noted for the sharp curves that the train had to negotiate) closed to passengers on 9 September 1963, although it remained open for milk traffic until 1 November 1975. Here 0-4-2T No 1450 waits with milk tanks on a Sunday afternoon in September 1964. This locomotive is now preserved on the Dart Valley Railway.

28 Stationmaster Fred Pugh strides down the platform on a tour of inspection, while in the background 1450 simmers at the platform with empty milk tanks for the factory. The steps under the water column seem to be inappropriate as the fireman usually climbed up the steps on the bunker. The stove with the long chimney was necessary in the winter to stop the water column from freezing up during the cold months.

29

30

29 Speen, with a 0-6-0PT arriving with a train from Newbury on 21 November 1959. Fine pieces of Great Westernalia are to be seen here. The crossing gates are hand operated and oil lit. When the gates are opened the lamp revolves showing the red light for obstruction. The steps up to the lamps enable the lampman to reach the socket when cleaning the glass. The GWR notice by the road may be observed (in chocolate and cream), 12 years after nationalisation! (R. Denison)

30 Speen again, this time the halt, of typical GWR pagoda-style construction. The lamp post had a ratchet for hauling up the oil lamp. This halt was typical of the many Great Western halts opened between the wars serving sparse areas.

31 Newbury West Fields, the first station out on the Newbury to Lambourne line, with pannier tank No 4670 arriving. The GWR auto-trailer car, as the saloon was termed, is of the prewar standard variety with drop-down steps and appears to be in GWR livery.

32

32 Lambourn, the terminus of the branch from Newbury. This photograph was taken shortly before closure of the line on 4 January 1960. The line was originally opened as the Lambourn Valley Railway in 1898, and was purchased by the GWR in 1905. Note the GWR seats and cashbox on the platform.

33 Winter shadows fall on the damp outline of Chipping Norton on the last day of operation, 12 December 1962. The line was once part of the GWR through-route from Kingham to Banbury. Weeds are starting to grow through the paving and birds have actually nested in the lamp.

34 Aberayron, terminus of the lengthy branch from Lampeter. 14XX class No 1419 in GWR livery with autocoach on the rear. This line closed on 12 February 1951.

33

34

35   Blenheim and Woodstock, the terminus of the short branch from Kidlington in Oxfordshire. The 0-4-2T has arrived with the autotrain from Kidlington and the locomotive has the passenger headlamp in position on the top bracket. The GWR lamp on the platform was of the late nineteenth-century GWR style. This line was typical of the short Great Western country branch, but closed on 1 March 1954.

No account of the British branch line scene would be complete without a mention of the activities of the one time Bishops Castle Railway in Shropshire – the most curious branch line in English railway history. The railway was a private company and ran from the junction of the Shrewsbury and Hereford line at Craven Arms to the small market town of Bishops Castle. The small company was spurned by the larger railways who did not wish to burden themselves with a moneyless concern. A noticeable feature of the Bishops Castle Railway was that it never paid a dividend on its share capital during the whole of its existence. The line was promoted originally as a through route to Wales, but the money ran out at Lydham Heath so a branch had to be built to Bishops Castle. This involved a reversal at the former point to enable the trains to get to the terminus.

36   The line's No 1 an 0-4-2T, built for GWR in 1869, a class well known on the GWR for branch line use. The locomotive was purchased by the Bishops Castle Railway in 1905 for £700 and was scrapped when the line closed in 1936. In this scene taken in the thirties, the mixed train has obviously been stopped for the photographers for a short while somewhere near Bishops Castle.

35

36

37 A brief moment in the late twenties or early thirties, at Lydham Heath, the point on the line where the train had to reverse to get to its destination at Bishops Castle. The locomotive, probably the 0-6-0 *Carlisle*, is running round the train which consisted of old six-wheel vehicles bought second hand from the GWR. Passengers in these vehicles had to keep their umbrellas up when there was rain as the roofs leaked so much!

38 The pride of the line was the
0-6-0 tender locomotive *Carlisle*,
seen here at Lydham Heath prior to
running round the train. The rails
seem to have been buried in the
grass! This locomotive was built in
1868 by Kitsons of Leeds, as an
0-6-0ST for Thomas Nelson, a
contractor in Carlisle, before being
bought second-hand by the BCR in
1895. Note that there are no balance
weights on the driving wheels, an
unusual feature. Of the company's
locomotives, only *No 1* (Fig 36) and
Carlisle survived at closure in 1936,
both being scrapped shortly afterwards. Picture taken shortly before
closure.

39 Plowden station in the winter
after closure and during demolition
of the line. Surprisingly, the station
still remains as a private house and is
very little altered in appearance to
this day.

40 Horderley, on the Bishops
Castle Railway, sees little business as
the weeds start to take over during
the final years of operation. The line
finally succumbed in 1936, shortly
after this picture was taken.

41   Another curious railway in Shropshire was the Shropshire and Montgomeryshire Light Railway, one of the Colonel Stephens group of light railways. This line had an eventful career, opening and closing as economic circumstances prevailed. It was originally the only part of the Potteries, Shrewsbury and North Wales Railway to be built, being opened from Shrewsbury to Blodwell with a branch from Kinnerley to Criggion in 1866. But it closed entirely in 1880 and lay derelict until 1907, when it was reconstructed under the provisions of the 1896 Light Railways Act, with Col H.F. Stephens as engineer. It reopened from Shrewsbury to Llanymynech (the junction with the Cambrian Railways) in 1911, with the name of Shropshire and Montgomeryshire Light Railway (but still known locally as 'The Pots'). The Criggion branch reopened in 1912. The terminus of the railway was at a station in Shrewsbury called 'The Abbey'. In this picture an LNWR goods 0-6-0 is simmering at the platform ready for departure to Kinnerley. The locomotive was purchased second hand from the LMS in 1932 and retained LMS lettering while on the S & M Railway. Note how the telegraph wires are mounted on the lamps.

42 The other end of the line from Shrewsbury took the traveller to Llanymynech, where the Shropshire and Montgomeryshire Light Railway joined up with the GWR main line. No 8236 shunts the train back into the platform after running round. The leading coach is of interest, having been built in 1848 as a royal saloon for the London and South Western Railway.

43 Special occasions on the Shropshire and Montgomeryshire Light Railway. The first picture shows a pre-war special with the diminutive locomotive *Gazelle* and four wheeled saloon. This outing, organised by the Birmingham Locomotive Club, shows *Gazelle* blowing off steam at Llanymynech Junction in 1939. The locomotive and coach were available for hire and local social organisations used them for outings. A quote from *The Shropshire & Montgomeryshire Railway* by E.S. Tonks gives some impression of what it was like to travel behind this unique contraption:

What memories – nostalgic yet happy – their recollection calls up! The grass grown track, the human chain of buckets from a pond at Criggion to help Driver Owen fill the tiny water tank through an inverted taper top can with bottom sawn off; the two cyclists who nearly fell off their machines at Llandrino Road at the incredible sight of the 'wooden engine' and coach and its compliment of laughing fellows.

Gazelle, reputed to be the smallest standard gauge steam locomotive on rails, was built in 1893 as a 2-2-2 by Dodman of King's Lynn. It was subsequently rebuilt as a 0-4-2 WT by W.G. Bagnall at Stafford, after purchase by the S & MLR from T. Ward of Sheffield in 1911. It has wooden wheels and a total weight of only $5\frac{1}{2}$ tons. It was purchased to work the Criggion branch in conjunction with an ex-LCC horse tramcar, as the infirm timbers of the Melverley viaduct (which had collapsed during the closed period 1880-1911) could not be relied upon to support any heavier combination. The four-wheel saloon shown was fabricated from the body of the middle coach of a withdrawn 1921 vintage three-car Ford railcar (built by Edmunds of Thetford), which was rebuilt onto the chassis of the horse tramcar. This combination of *Gazelle* and hybrid four-wheel saloon worked all passenger trains during 1934-9, after regular passenger traffic ceased in 1934. *Gazelle* was preserved on a plinth at Longmoor, the depot of the Royal Corps of Transport, but can now be seen at the National Railway Museum, York.

44 Nearly twenty years later on the same system, this time on the Criggion branch, which by some curious quirk of reorganisation had found its way into Western Region ownership. On this occasion a special expedition set out from Shrewsbury on 21 September 1958 and the Criggion branch was traversed, this time by a petrol-driven inspection vehicle, the tour being organised by the Stephenson Locomotive Society. The view here shows Melverley, one of the intermediate stations, just as it was built by the Potteries, Shrewsbury and North Wales Railway in 1871. The track, which was the original from when the line was built in 1871, was double-headed bull head type which had disappeared on normal running lines by the turn of the century. Double-headed rail could be turned when worn on the top surface, but the practice grew out of fashion as the worn rail-section tended to score the chairs.

45 Shropshire and Montgomeryshire motive power in its heyday.
The 0-6-0 goods *Hesperus* of ex-
London and South Western origin in
spruced up appearance on the S &
MLR in prewar days. This
locomotive was built in April 1875
by Beyer Peacock, reboilered with an
Adams boiler at Nine Elms in 1888,
and sold to the Shropshire and
Montgomeryshire Light Railway in
1911. It lasted until 1941. Note the
lack of balance weights on the
driving wheels. The S & MLR was
taken over by the Army during
World War II and finally closed
down in 1958, having been used by
the military until that time. *(Real
Photographs Co Ltd)*

London Transport

The Brill branch closed on 2 December 1935 and was an unusual byway being worked by the Metropolitan Railway's 4-4-0 tanks built by Beyer Peacock and very typical of that builder's design. The line was owned jointly by the Metropolitan Railway and the London and North-Eastern Railway and would in today's terms be operated by London Transport and British Rail. The pictures here are of one station on the line and depict the gradual change in the line's fortunes.

46   Three photographs of Westcott showing the changing scene from the same location. In the first picture a Metropolitan 4-4-0 is arriving at an empty platform.

47   The railway in its final years before closure in 1935, with a Metropolitan 4-4-0 tank, an example of which is now preserved in the London Transport Museum at Syon Park.

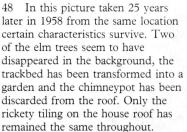

48   In this picture taken 25 years later in 1958 from the same location certain characteristics survive. Two of the elm trees seem to have disappeared in the background, the trackbed has been transformed into a garden and the chimneypot has been discarded from the roof. Only the rickety tiling on the house roof has remained the same throughout.

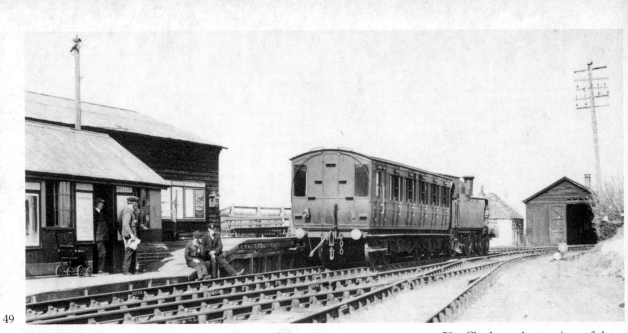

49

50 Chesham, the terminus of the short branch from Chalfont with a Great Central Railway 4-4-2T. This line still survives as an electrified branch. In this picture taken in June 1956 the three coach push-and-pull set is shown behind the engine. The coaching stock was a curious survival from the nineteenth century and eventually found a home on the Bluebell Railway in Sussex.

49 Brill terminus in 1933 with Metropolitan tank locomotive No 23. The crew prepare to work the return train to Quainton Road and the driver is checking the time by his watch. The extension to Stanmore, now part of the Bakerloo line of London Transport, seems to be the news of the moment, judging from the comments on the poster! *(H. C. Casserley)*

50

London Midland Region (LMS Group)

51   A London and North Western Railway branch line scene at Buckingham on a Saturday in 1959. 41275 has just arrived with the push-and-pull from Verney Junction, with a connection from Bletchley and the train will propel on to Banbury (Merton St). Notice the LMS nameboard and the L & NWR gaslamps, quite a busy scene for a line that closed to Banbury on 2 January 1961. This scene was used in British Railways publicity posters in the early sixties, albeit with a diesel multiple-unit, to publicise modern branch line travel!

52 Daventry, on the Weedon to Leamington line. A class 2 tank pauses en route in this large station with no passengers and even less freight in August 1958. The all wooden structure was built to accommodate far larger crowds. In the days prior to grouping, in the pre-plastic and synthetic-material age the cheap materials used for building construction had to be timber. Notice the L & NWR bridge plate, still standard today and of a type still used by London Midland region of BR on modern bridge structures. At this period LMS station nameboards (left) were commonplace.

53 A fleeting glimpse from a passing train of Knapton & Stockton, on the Weedon to Leamington branch. Just for one moment the camera catches the rural atmosphere of a declining railway in the late fifties. Notice how the drainpipe terminates in the bucket, the Midland Red bus timetable on the wall (a company with railway associations) and the LMS oil lamp. The closure notice of the line is displayed for 15 September 1958, just two weeks after the picture was taken. These buildings were of a temporary construction, having been erected by the L & NWR prior to grouping, with provision for a more permanent structure to replace them. The canopy over the station clock to protect it from the vagaries of the weather may be noted; all L & NWR clocks kept Crewe time, synchronized daily by order of the General Manager!

54 Llanarthney in Wales, an outpost of the L & NWR system in the west in 1962. By the time that this picture had been taken the Western Region had taken over the lines in Wales and a process of Westernisation had taken place, hence the pannier tank. This was a really rural line which had changed little from the grouping. Llanarthney and Drysllwyn were on the Llandilo to Carmarthen branch of the L & NWR Central Wales line. Llanarthney became an unstaffed halt from January 1954, and closed for goods in June 1959 and the line closed completely on 9 September 1963, at the height of the Beeching purge.

54

55 Drysllwyn, an outpost on the
L & NWR Central Wales line, sees
little activity at any time of the day.
It became an unstaffed halt during
World War II, but was restaffed
afterwards.

56 Redwharf Bay, in Anglesey, the
terminus of the winding branch from
Bangor. This line closed to passengers in September 1930, but
freight lasted until the fifties. A
typical L & NWR wooden building
is seen here, gradually disappearing
into the undergrowth, receding back
into nature and oblivion. (*A.F.E. Field*)

57 A London and North Western Railway country station at Kinnerton, on the borders of Flintshire and Cheshire, a few days before closure. The nameboard posts of L & NWR pattern also hold the oil lamp, there being no electricity supply. The nameboard precedes the platform, warning the passenger of the station's impending arrival.

The author arrived here having hitch-hiked from Mold in a bread van. Negotiations with the late-turn gaffer, who was locking up the booking office after going off duty, produced an L & NWR single ticket to the next station. This was one of the last pre-grouping tickets to be on sale in Britain, albeit some 40 years after the company had ceased to exist. The line closed three days later on 30 April 1962.

58 Dead end for an LMS class 3F 0-6-0T from Willesden shed. The location is believed to be Hammersmith and Chiswick station, terminus of a short London branch line from South Acton. This line was operated by a rail motor designed by Mr Whale of the L & NWR. The branch terminus, which was in use as a coal depot in recent years, closed to passengers in 1916. A curious feature of this $1\frac{1}{4}$ mile long line was that it contained three intermediate halts.

59 This photograph was not taken in 1909 as the scene might suggest, but in 1958 when L & NWR 0-6-0 Webb saddle tanks were still in use at Wolverton Carriage Works, and the locomotives shown had departmental Nos CD3, CD6 and CD7. The 2P 4-4-0 No 40421 had just come off a special from London. The Webb 0-6-0 tank locomotives were used to take over the special train for a jaunt up the Newport Pagnell branch. The locomotive detailed to do the work did in fact run out of breath en route having to stop for a 'blow up' because of the unusual load.

57

60 The Locomotive Club of Great Britain had enough wisdom to arrange a special train with an L & NWR saddle tank on the Newport Pagnell branch in June 1958. Although an L & NWR engine on an L & NWR line the load was too much for the ageing saddle tank No CD7, which had to stop for a 'blow up' en route to raise steam.

61 Rotton Park Road, one of the stations on the L & NWR Harborne branch, taken shortly before closure in November 1934. This is a good example of an L & NWR town branch. Notice the typical L & NWR signals on wooden posts and the L & NWR trespass notice at the end of the platform.

62

62 A quiet moment on the Harborne branch with an L & NWR coal tank. The fireman has got down to couple up the locomotive after having run round the train.

63 Holywell Town, the terminus of the short but picturesque line from Holywell Junction in Flintshire. Brisk business for the LMS rail push-and-pull unit in 1953, one year prior to closure. *(H.C. Casserley)*

63

64

64 Cheadle, one of the last North Staffordshire Railway branches to survive into the sixties. A class 4 tank prepares to depart for Stoke with an empty passenger train on 25 July 1961. This line closed to passengers on 17 June 1963.

65 Coniston, in the Lake district. This was the terminus of the scenic branch from Foxfield. By the time that this picture had been taken the line was on its last legs. Freight traffic had almost vanished and the trains were running practically empty. Although the signalling here has been standardised, a noticeable feature about the furniture is the Furness Railway seat with the 'squirrel' in the ironwork. All Furness stations had these ironwork seats, several of which have found their way into the National Railway Museum. The superb overall roof here survived to the end in October 1958. The railwayman is carrying a single-line tablet contained in a standard carrying satchel with a large loop for manual tablet exchange, for the driver's return to Foxfield.

66 Middleton, the short Lancashire branch from Middleton Junction, in LMS days. Class 4 No 2282 arrives at the stops. This line survived until 7 September 1964 in spite of bus competition. How the station buildings have deteriorated – no glass, loose paving and no customers! The LMS had little money to spare on suburban branches in the post-war period.

65

66

67

67 Barnoldswick, known locally as 'Barney', was a curious little branch. When this photograph was taken the town was in Lancashire, but now because of a county boundary reshuffle, the town is in Yorkshire! Barnoldswick was part of the former Midland system and was an outpost in the Lancashire and Yorkshire area. The feature about this line was the fact that the station was built across the public highway and the engines had to run round the train by crossing the road, much to the annoyance of the motorists. The famous Midland signal can just be discerned above the locomotive and is the revolving crossbar type. The line closed on 27 September 1965. When this picture was taken in 1962 the signalman was wearing wooden clogs.

68 The Midland branch to Leicester West Bridge. The first railway to Leicester opened as early as July 1832 as the Leicester and Swannington Railway, the first line on which the steam whistle was used. Shortly after leaving Leicester the line plunged into a dead straight tunnel of one mile in length. The tunnel had no man-hole recesses so that it was not advisable to be caught in the tunnel when a train was about. Passenger services finished in September 1928, although goods lasted until the sixties. In this picture of the new West Bridge Station erected in 1893 the Midland branch train can be seen in all its magnificence. The 0-6-0 goods with six-wheel coaches seems to have been pushed right back on to the buffers so that the posed picture of the staff can be taken. A fine example of a Midland six-wheeled vehicle can be seen in the National Railway Museum.

69 Glenfield, on the Leicester We Bridge line. This scene shows typic Midland characteristics, the signal i the background with a long spike is very Midland as is also the station nameboard, set back at an angle to be read by passengers of approachir trains. This system was exported to colonial railways in the last century and Argentina particularly, where the Midland style of nameboard survives.

68

69

70

71

70 Higham Ferrers, Northampton-shire, a short Midland branch which ended up in the middle of nowhere from Wellingborough. The line was built as a main line and was intended to go on to Market Harborough, but as the rival L & NWR beat the Midland to it there was no point in continuing the line beyond this point. The line closed on 16 June 1959.

71 Midland architecture on the Nailsworth branch at Woodchester. A great deal of timber has been used in the construction of this small country station. Although passenger services ceased on 8 June 1949, goods lasted until the sixties. When this picture was taken the train ran twice a week to Nailsworth. Notice the angle fencing, a feature of Midland and LMS structures.

72 Cam, on the short branch to Dursley in Gloucestershire. A lack of paint seems to be the noticeable feature of this station on this short branch of the former Midland Railway. The station is in the former LMS livery — what is left of it! Trains ceased to call on 10 September 1962, when the line closed. The lamp is the standard Midland-type with two rings at the base of a six-sided column.

Eastern Region (L & NER Group)

73

73   Leicester Belgrave Road was a Great Northern Railway incursion into Midland territory. The GNR opened up a station of large dimensions to rival the Midland Railway edifice down the road in the town. Unfortunately the terminus was not very useful because the lines served did not go anywhere in particular, except for Skegness and Mablethorpe. The station was ideally situated for the Sunday excursions to Skegness for day trippers and in its last days passenger trains ran on Sundays only! Here a B1 4-6-0 is about to start with an excursion to Skegness. Notice the GNR somer-sault signals on the right mounted on concrete posts. These 'ghost' trains ran until 9 September 1962, the normal passenger service having been discontinued in December 1953.

74   The same train in pre-war days. A Great Northern Railway 4-4-0 (D3) in spotless apple green and a row of GNR vehicles trailing behind, mostly six-wheeled, and all in varnished teak.

75   Ryhall and Belmisthorpe, the intermediate station on the Essendine to Stamford branch in Rutland, which closed on 15 June 1959.

74

75

76 A Great Northern relic at Ramsey North photographed in April 1957.

77 Kelvedon Low Level, the terminus of the light railway to Tollesbury Pier in Essex. This ex-Great Eastern line used special coaches to enable people to board the trains at ground level. Where the Great Western would have steps lowered for rail-level halts the GER preferred to have lower coaches, giving them a distinct American appearance. This line opened in 1904 as a light railway, and closed to passengers in May 1951. The leading vehicle No 60461, which came from the Wisbeach and Upwell railway, was the actual coach used later in the film *The Titfield Thunderbolt.* (*J.H. Meredith*)

78   Feering Halt, on the Tollesbury
line with an old bus body as a
shelter for passengers in August
1950. The GER six-wheeled coach
at the front of the train was built in
1896 and came from the Stoke Ferry
branch, while the vehicle on the
right was the famous bogie saloon
used in *The Titfield Thunderbolt*.
Locomotive J67 0-6-0T No 68616.
(*J.H. Meredith*)

79   The engine shed at Kelvedon
with a GER 0-6-0T of J67 class
known by the railway staff as 'Buck
Jumpers'. The locomotive has been
garlanded for the occasion of the last
train on 5 May 1951 and has a
wreath on the side tank.

80

80 The engine shed at Thaxted, with J67 class 0-6-0T moving up for water. The GER used to mount their lamps on old rails, in this case for coaling at night or in winter. This photograph was taken on 23 August 1952, only three weeks before closure. Thaxted was the terminus of a Great Eastern Railway branch from Elsenham on the GER Liverpool Street to Cambridge main line, north of Bishops Stortford. (*J.H. Meredith*)

81 Another Great Eastern branch was the line to Framlingham in Suffolk, which closed on 3 November 1952. This view in July shows GER 2-4-2T locomotive of class F6 introduced in 1911 for branch line work. The train is mixed and the cramped layout of Framlingham station does not give much room for manoeuvre. The coaches are ex-GER main line vehicles painted in the unimaginative dun brown of the L & NER secondary line stock. (*J.H. Meredith*)

82 Aldeburgh, the Great Eastern branch that survived until 12 September 1966. In this picture the overall roof is still in use, later demolished when the line became dieselised and the train had to propel backwards to run round the loop.

83

84

83 Haven House, on the Skegness branch, looking towards the crossing. The Great Northern Railway was famous for the use of the somersault signal, as was also the Midland and Great Northern Joint Railway and the Midland Northern Counties Committee in Ireland. Here at Haven House in Lincolnshire the starter is in the 'off' position and the gates closed across the road. A train is due, coming up from behind the photographer – a very dangerous situation to be in. Great Northern signals still survive in remote parts of Lincolnshire, the most prized specimen being the Wainfleet up-distant which has the spectacle and lamp mounted part-way down the post while the arm is at the top.

84 Fockerby, on the joint line from Reedness Junction, in the damp mists of the Humber. The Lancashire and Yorkshire Railway 0-6-0 has pushed the train back for the photographer. This remote outpost of the NER and Lancashire and Yorkshire, Axholme Joint Railway closed on 17 July 1933. Here in this pre-grouping view the crew pose for the photographer and traffic seems to be light, the Lancashire and Yorkshire fencing seems to suffice, there being no station buildings in sight to accommodate passengers.

85 The Wensleydale line from Northallerton to Garsdale was one of the longest branches on the North Eastern Region, being 39¾ miles from end to end. The line was opened throughout on 10 October 1878 by the North Eastern Railway to Hawes and by the Midland Railway to Garsdale on the newly completed Settle to Carlisle line (Garsdale was known as Hawes Junction in pre-grouping days). This trans-Pennine line crossed some wild country and was often snowed up during winter. The passenger service was discontinued on 26 April 1954. The daily freight train to Hawes is shown here in March 1959 hauled by no less an engine than K1 class No 62005, now to be seen running on the North Yorkshire Moors Railway. This view was taken at Finghall Lane, part of the original York, Newcastle and Berwick Railway branch line to Leyburn, the sound stonework of the station being in that company's style. The branch from Hawes to Garsdale ceased to carry passengers from 13 March 1959.

86 The station building at Constable Burton on the Wensleydale line, as seen from the daily goods. The stepped stonework on the gable ends of the station roof is similar in design to that at Finghall Lane. The North Eastern Railway influence is apparent with the lamps on their wooden standards and the footstep for the lamp lighter. The buildings are still in North Eastern Region colours, the line having been closed to passengers five years earlier in April 1954.

87 The Wear Valley Railway was an extremely lengthy branch which wound its way up through the hills from Bishop Auckland to the Pennines at Wearhead. In this picture a J39 class 0-6-0 shunts the sidings with minerals at Stanhope, the principal station on the line, a cold and frosty November morning in 1960 providing ideal photographic conditions.

88 Stanhope again, this time with the J39 blowing off steam and the irresistable temptation to work the vintage North Eastern slotted lower-quadrant signal into the picture. The passenger service on this line finished on 29 June 1953, freight lasting much longer.

89

89 Wolsingham, with the daily
freight en route to Weardale pausing
to pick up any odd wagons available
in the sidings in November 1960.

90 Alston, the epitome of the
North Eastern branch in the early
fifties with a North Eastern Region
orange nameboard, now a thing of
the past. The G5 0-4-4T is on
L & NER stock, which may be artic-
ulated, tucked away under the
overall roof, now alas demolished.
Notice the one-road engine house
next door to the station, North
Eastern practice being to stable
locomotives out on the branches
where there may be trouble in winter
months through 'snowing in' of
trains.

91 Alston, this time in 1958, with
the line being worked by a standard
class 3 locomotive. This was a rare
class as only twenty locomotives
were built; these 2-6-0 tender
locomotives were designed at
Swindon in 1954. The buildings
were typical of the solid and magnificent structures of the one-time
Newcastle and Carlisle Railway. This
line miraculously survived until 1976
there being no way over the river
South Tyne at Lambley by road, but
closure took place in May 1976.

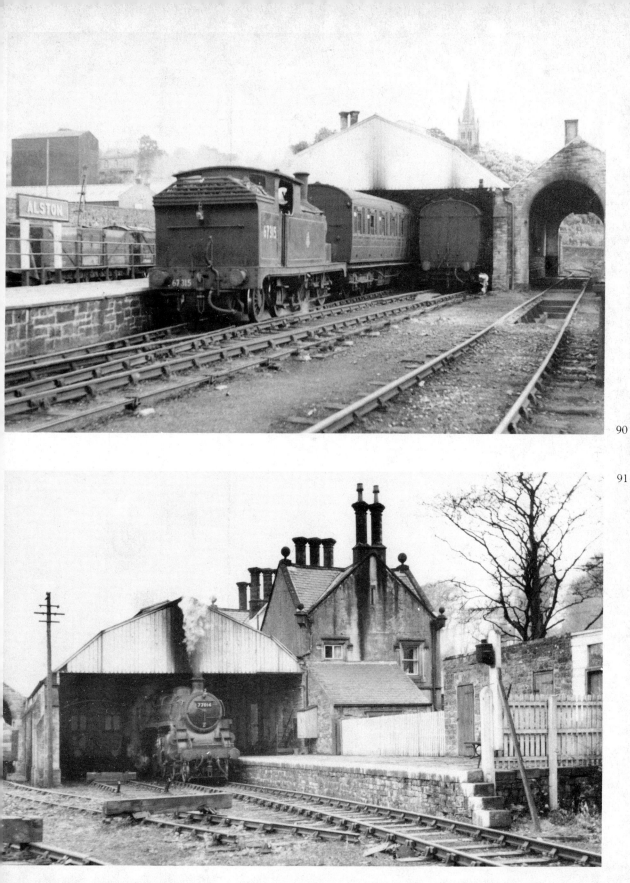

90

91

92 Seahouses, on the North Sunderland Railway possessed one of the curious North Eastern Railway Y7 class 0-4-0T locomotives, built in 1897. A Y7 locomotive (ex-NER No 985) has now been preserved. The line was 4 miles long and ran from Chathill on the East Coast main line to Seahouses on the coast. The line was worked by the L & NER from 1939, having been opened in 1898. British Railways closed it on 29 October 1951.

94 The daily goods climbs out of Chapelhall, hauled by Caledonian 0-6-0 No 57592 in 1963. The Airdrie to Newhouse branch in the Clyde Valley was closed to passengers as long ago as 1 December 1930. *(R. Hamilton)*

Scottish Region

93 Balnerno, an unusual line situated on a loop on the Edinburgh to Carstairs main line of the former Caledonian Railway. The passenger service ceased on 1 November 1943, but the freight traffic lasted for several years afterwards. On this occasion (1962) a special train has been organised utilising a class 2 standard tender locomotive, with the Caledonian coaches (now preserved) being used. The permanent way gang seem to be oblivious to the extraordinary event of a passenger train, very rare at this period as the service finished over twenty years before. The coaches still survive at the Scottish Preservation Society HQ in Falkirk.

95   A North British line with NBR
engine. The Leslie branch in
Fifeshire with a railtour special in
1963 hauled by J37 class No 64618.
This line lost its passenger service on
4 January 1932. Note the NBR lamp
on the platform.

96 A goods train, which ran three times a week, stops to shunt at Wigtown on this lengthy line to Whithorn in August 1960. An outpost of the Portpatrick and Wigtownshire Joint Railway, it is now abandoned, leaving a large part of Scotland in the south-west without railways. This railway was owned jointly by the L & NW, Midland, Caledonian and Glasgow & South Western Railways and operated with CR and G & SWR locomotives and stock until absorbed by the LMS at grouping.

97 The famous ex-North British
Railway 4-4-0 locomotive *Glen
Douglas* rounding a bend on the
short Methven branch of the
Caledonian Railway in Perthshire,
one of the shortest on the system.
The occasion is a railtour organised
by the Branch Line Society on 23
April 1962. This locomotive (L &
NER class D34) was preserved in
original NBR colours and with the
three others ran specials around
Scotland in the early sixties, until
taken out of service in 1965 and
moved to Glasgow Transport
Museum the following year.

98 A J36 class near Blanefield, crossing the road on the Aberfoyle branch in 1958 with a Stephenson Locomotive Society special. Note the earth-ballasted track.

99   A sombre occasion at Lauder, the terminus of the Lauder Light Railway. The regular service to passengers closed on 12 September 1932, but freight lingered on until after the war, when the service was worked by tender-tank locomotives – a rare arrangement for a British line. On this occasion the very last train, organised by the Branch Line Society, is hauled by a class 2 BR standard 2-6-0. Crowds gather to watch the press photograph the occasion on 15 November 1958.

100   One of the other preserved engines in Scotland was the Great North of Scotland Railway 4-4-0 *Gordon Highlander*, known by Scotsmen as 'the soldier'. This ex-LNER D40 class was painted in GNSR green livery, but sceptics doubted whether the locomotive had ever been painted in these colours as it had been built so near the 1923 grouping. This locomotive, along with the other Scottish preserved specimens, now reposes in the Glasgow Transport Museum. To see it working flat out on the old Great North branches in the 1960s was a sight not easily forgotten. This picture shows No 49, as it had become, hard at work on the Macduff branch between Rothienorman and Wartle with a joint Branch Line Society and Stephenson Locomotive Society railtour on 21 April 1962.

101

101 Turriff with GNSR No 49, here restored, pulling away after a water stop. The Macduff branch, a long winding and hilly line in Aberdeenshire, had lost its passenger service on 1 October 1951. Just look at that GNSR signal, which the train seems to have ignored! The line was probably being worked on the 'one engine in steam' principle.

102 Blackstone Junction, with the 'Jones Goods' resplendent in Highland Railway yellow livery seen propelling down the Linwood branch on 17 April 1965. This type of locomotive was designed by David Jones, the Highland Railway locomotive superintendent during 1870-96. These were the first British 4-6-0 locomotives when introduced in 1894.

102

103 The Jones Goods at Inverness takes water before setting out on a tour of Scottish lines on 21 April 1962.

104 Highland Railway No 103, the Jones Goods, passes Gollanfield Junction, site of the abandoned Fort George Branch, on 21 April 1962. No 103 was the first tender loco-motive in the country built by Sharp Stewart in 1894. In 1959 this engine was restored to full working order and used on special trains. The Fort George branch lost its passenger service in 1943, but lingered on for freight until the late fifties.

105 and 106   Before and after views of the terminus at Fort Augustus, on the shores of Loch Ness. The line started life as the Invergarry and Fort Augustus Railway, an independent railway. The line of 24 miles in length through the Highlands was an expensive project, and the cost of construction was so great that the railway could not afford locomotives or rolling stock! The Highland Railway came to the rescue and worked the line with their stock. The line opened in 1903 and was one of the first railways to be built utilising concrete, which has shown a remarkable durability in surviving 60 years where most other materials have perished. Judging by the Highland Railway locomotive this photograph was taken between 1903 and 1907, before operation was taken over by the North British Railway; possibly this picture was taken at the opening of the line.

Isle of Man

107 St Johns, on the Isle of Man Railway with 2-4-0T No 5 *Mona* (built by Beyer Peacock in 1874) preparing to back out with a train for Douglas in 1958. St Johns was formerly the centre of the system being the junction for Peel, Ramsey and Foxdale. The Isle of Man Railway, a narrow gauge gem, in recent years has had probably the most chequered career of any railway. Since 1967 Manx people have never been quite sure whether their railway would reopen the following season or not. During 1975 the service ran from Castletown to Port Erin, and for 1976 the Manx Parliament has insisted that the track from Ballasalla to Douglas remain in situ. During the 1976 season services are scheduled to run from Ballasalla to Port Erin. Douglas Station, although now a sorry sight, remains intact. On the other hand St Johns has been abandoned and gorse bushes thrive where trains once plied their way to Douglas.

The Isle of Man Railway equipment has been put up for sale by auction in April 1977.

108

108   At Ramsey No 14 (one of the ex-Manx Northern engines) sizzles at the end of the platform in May 1958. *Thornhill*, with one of the famous bell-shaped domes of the Victorian period, is one of the original Beyer Peacock 2-4-0T locomotives painted out in the famous deep-brown livery of the post-war period.

109   Douglas station with No 14 again being prepared for the road in 1958. This rare survival of the Victorian age could have been photographed nearly a hundred years ago. The locomotive has a wooden buffer-beam, chain couplings and

inclined cylinders. Formerly No 3 of the Manx Northern Railway she was built in 1880 and reboilered in 1921, the last to be fitted with Salter valves, the rest of the engine being the original.

109

110 A magnificent line-up outside Douglas shed, showing locomotives of varying ages, but all 2-4-0s! The Manx standard gauge was 3ft 0in and the whole system was unique.

111 No 8 *Fennella* (Beyer Peacock, 1894) pulls away from one of the later 2-4-0s at Douglas station. The coaching stock was as rare as the motive power, all-bogie coaches were used on passenger trains but some of the coaches consisted of two ex-six-wheeled vehicles joined together.

Ireland

HORSE VAN, FINTONA

112 Fintona, scene of the famous
horse tram, in which the author,
unable to find suitable accommodation in the town, spent the night.
The trackbed was covered with
cinders so that the 'motive power'
could walk easily. The line was a
mere half mile long and ran from
Fintona to Fintona Junction.

113 Dick, the branch horse waiting
for the 'right away' at Fintona
Station. The station had an overall
roof, thus protection for incumbents
– man, beast, and trains – from the
elements was assured. (*M. Jose*)

114 The horse tram en route to Fintona, with Dick plodding uphill with the morning passenger. This photograph, taken on 18 September 1957, shows the steepness of the gradient on the line. The goods on the branch was worked by a locomotive, which had to work in the small hours of the morning so as not to scare the horse. When the horse-drawn vehicle arrived at Fintona Junction Dick was uncoupled and run light to the shed where he was locked up, in case he bolted from the steam locomotive of the arriving train. The line, alas, closed down on 1 October 1957, but the tramcar is now preserved in the Belfast Transport Museum. This tram had the only hay-burning, non-super-heated, quadruped power unit in the British Isles!

115 Valentia Harbour claimed to be the most westerly station in Europe. This long winding mountain line in the extreme south-west of Ireland has now passed on. The line had two trains per day and closed shortly after this photograph was taken in 1958.

116 Killorglin on the Valentina harbour branch in June 1961. On the left is locomotive No 133, a J15 (or to be correct 101) class 0-6-0 of ex-Great Southern & Western Railway vintage, which was from a very large class of 0-6-0s dating back in design to the 1870s. Demolition is in progress on this once-famous branch. Most of the equipment is permanent way material, which has been taken from the branch and stacked for disposal. The overall roof spans one track only, but an additional platform has been provided for crossing trains.

117 Kenmare, another remote branch through wild and mountainous countryside. Here is locomotive No 133 again with a mixed train to Kenmare Junction, in June 1958. The train is pre-grouping (the Irish grouping was in 1925), the leading vehicle being a Midland Great Western Railway corridor compartment coach with a GS & WR van (six-wheeled) behind, then a collection of goods vehicles. Most of the pre-1925 passenger stock was gas lit.

118 The monthly train to Tullow stops briefly at Dunlavin with the cattle special hauled by 0-6-0 No 171, a reboilered 101 class. The infrequent passing of trains meant that the vegetation had plenty of opportunity to get a hold on the track, and in some places the track was not visible under the weeds.

119 Tullow, with its monthly train, which on this occasion happened to be the last to run on the line as it was closed from this day 15 March 1959.

120 Geashill, on the MGWR line from Portarlington to Athlone, with locomotive 588, a large boilered MGWR 0-6-0. This was a well-kept country station with little traffic and even less revenue. The oil lamp bracket is empty, the lamps burners being inserted at dusk by the station staff from the lamp room. At many remote stations the duty of lighting the stations lamps was performed by the guard as instructed in the working timetable.

121 The Ballaghaderreen branch train could have come straight out of the nineteenth century, had it not been for the electric light on the platform. In this 1959 picture of No 655, an MGWR 2-4-0, the train is about to set off to Kilfree Junction. The train consists of all six-wheeled stock and consisted of one composite vehicle formerly housing passengers in three classes. The two rear coaches date from the 1880s. *(G. Blacklock)*

122 Edmondstown Station with signals for trains travelling in either direction. This two-way signal dates from when the line opened in the nineteenth century. It was one of the two stations on the Ballaghaderreen branch. The flat-bottom broad-gauge track seems to be well cleared of weeds, and almost of ballast!

123 The Timoleague and Court-macsherry Railway was a roadside tramway which, apart from occasional summer seaside day excursions, only had trains in winter for the seasonal sugar beet traffic. This view in winter 1960 shows MGWR 0-6-0 No 552 with a very light train of empties. The line closed down completely in April 1961.

Appendix

The Beeching Report was published at 12.00 hours on 27 March 1963. Most of the proposals in the report have since been implemented and large areas of the British Isles are now without railways. This appendix lists all passenger lines on British Railways closed since 1 January, 1963, and includes main lines as well as branches, but excludes small curves. From this date onwards the rural passenger railway was finally doomed.

Line	Region/ Company of Origin	Date Closed
Abbeyhill (Jcn) – Piershill (Jcn)	SC/NB	7.9.64
Aberdare (Low Level) – Abercynon	W/TV	16.3.64
Aberfeldy – Ballinluig	SC/HR	3.5.65
Aberystwyth – Strata Florida	W/GW	14.12.64
Abingdon – Radley	W/GW	9.9.63
Accrington – Ramsbottom	LM/LY	5.12.66
Afon Wen – Caernarvon	LM/LNW	7.12.64
Aldeburgh – Saxmundham	E/GE	12.9.66
Alloa – Kinross Jcn	SC/NB	15.6.64
Alloa – Larbert	SC/CR	29.1.68
Alnmouth – Alnwick	E/NER	29.1.68
Alston – Haltwhistle	NE/NER	1.5.76
Alton – Winchester	S/LSW	5.2.73
Amlwch – Gaerwen	LM/LNW	7.12.64
Andover Jcn – Romsey	S/LSW	.7.9.64
Ardrossan (Montgomere Pier) – Stevenston	SC/GSW	26.9.67
Ardsley – Laisterdyke (via Morley Top)	NE/GN	4.7.66
Ardsley – Castleford	NE/MJ	2.11.64
Arthington – Burley-In-Wharfdale	NE/NER	22.3.65
Aschurch – Redditch	W/MID	1.10.62 *
Athelney – Durston	W/GW	15.6.64
Athelney – Yeovil Town	W/GW	15.6.64
Audley End – Bartlow	E/GE	7.9.64
Aviemore – Forres	SC/HR	18.10.65
Aylesbury – Rugby (Central)	LM/GC	5.9.66
Banbury – Woodford Halse	LM/GC	5.9.66
Backworth – Hartley	NE/NER	2.11.64
Bacup – Rawtenstall	LM/LY	5.12.66
Bala – Bala Jcn	LM/GW	18.1.65
Ballachulish – Connel Ferry	SC/CR	28.3.66
Ballater – Aberdeen (Ferryhill Jcn)	SC/GNS	28.2.66
Banbury (Jcn) – Woodford Halse (Culworth Jcn)	LM/GC	5.9.66
Banff – Tillynaught	SC/GNS	6.7.64
Barassie – Kilmarnock	SC/GSW	3.3.69
Barnard Castle – Darlington	NE/NER	30.11.64
Barnoldswick – Earby	LM/MID	27.9.65
Barnsley (Exchange Jcn) – Penistone (Barnsley Jcn)	E/GC	5.1.70
Barnsley (Quarry Jcn) – Mexborough	E/GC	5.1.70
Barnstaple Jcn – Torrington	W/LSW	4.10.65
Barnstaple Jcn – Taunton	W/GW	3.10.66

*official closure date 17.6.63

Barry – Bridgend	W/BRY	15.6.64
Barry Pier – Barry Island	W/BRY	12.10.71
Bath (Green Park) – Mangotsfield	W/MID	7.3.66
Bath (Green Park) – Poole	W/SD	7.3.66
Bedford St Johns – Cambridge	LM/LNW	1.1.68
Bere Alston – Okehampton	W/LSW	6.5.68
Berkeley Road – Sharpness	W/SWV	2.11.64
Berkswell – Kenilworth	LM/LNW	18.1.65
Beverley – York	NE/NER	29.11.65
Bewdley – Hartlebury	LM/GW	5.1.70
Bewdley – Kidderminster	LM/GW	5.1.70
Bewdley – Shrewsbury (Sutton Bridge Jcn)	LM/GW	9.9.63
(Bewdley – Bridgnorth is now part of the Severn Valley Railway)		
Bexhill West – Crowhurst	S/SEC	15.6.64
Birkenhead Woodside – Rock Ferry	LM/BJ	5.11.67
Birmingham (Moor St Jcn) – Snow Hill	LM/GW	4.3.68
Birmingham (Snow Hill) – Wolverhampton (Low Level)	LM/GW	6.3.72
Bishop Auckland – Durham	NE/NER	4.5.64
Bishop Auckland – Crook	NE/NER	8.3.65
Blackpool Ctl – South	LM/PWY	2.11.64
Blackpool South – Kirkham (direct line)	LM/PWY	7.9.64
Blackrod – Daisy Hill	LM/LY	6.9.65
Bletchley – Oxford	LM/LNW	1.1.68
Blowers Green – Old Hill	LM/GW	15.6.64
Blyth – Monkseaton	NE/NER	2.11.64
Boat of Garten – Craigellachie	SC/GNS	18.10.65
Bodmin North – Padstow	W/LSW	30.1.67
Bodmin Road – Boscarne Jcn	W/GW	30.1.67
Bogside (Byrehill Jcn) – Stevenson (Dubbs Jcn)	SC/GSW	6.4.64
Bolton-on-Dearne – Mexborough	NE/S & K	5.4.65
Bolton (East Jcn) – Rochdale	LM/LY	5.10.70
Boston – Peterborough	E/GN	5.10.70
(Spalding – Peterborough reopened 7.6.71)		
Boston – Woodhall Jcn	E/GN	17.6.63
Bourne End – High Wycombe	W/GW	4.5.70
Bournemouth West – Branksome	S/LSW	6.9.65
Bowling Jcn – Laisterdyke (West Jcn)	E/GN	9.6.69
Bradford-on-Avon – Chippenham	W/GW	18.4.66
Bramley – Laisterdyke (via Pudsey)	NE/GN	15.6.64
Bridgend – Cymmer Afan	W/GW	22.6.70
Bridgeton Cross – Newton (via Carmyle)	SC/CAL	5.10.64
Brighouse – Mirfield	E/LY	5.1.70
Brightlingsea – Wivenhoe	E/GE	15.6.64
Bristol (Temple Meads) – Yate	W/MID	27.12.69
Bridport – Maiden Newton	W/GW	5.5.75
Brixham – Churston	W/GW	13.5.63
Broadstone – Bath (Green Park)	S/SD	7.3.66
Broadstone – Brockenhurst (via Ringwood)	S/LSW	4.5.64
Broadstone – Hamworthy Jcn	S/LSW	4.5.64
Broadstone – Poole	S/LSW	7.3.66
Brocklesby – Ulceby	E/GC	6.5.68
Bromyard – Leominster Jcn (Worcester)	W/GW	7.9.64
Buckingham – Verney Jcn	LM/LNW	7.9.64
Bude – Okehampton	W/LSW	3.10.66
Buntingford – St Margarets	E/GE	16.11.64
Burton-on-Trent – Leicester (Knighton North)	LM/MID	7.9.64
Burton-on-Trent – Walsall	LM/MID	18.1.65
Burton Salmon – Castleford Central	E/NER	5.1.70
Bury (Bolton St) – Rawtenstall	LM/LY	5.6.72

Bury (Bolton St) – Clifton Jcn	LM/LY	5.12.66
Bury (Knowsley St) – Bolton	LM/LY	5.10.70
Bury (Knowsley St) – Rochdale	LM/LY	5.10.70
Buxton – Matlock/Chinley	LM/MID	6.3.67
Cadoxton (Biglis Jcn) – Penarth	W/TV	6.5.68
Caernarvon – Avon Wen	LM/LNW	7.12.64
Caernarvon – Bangor	LM/LNW	5.1.70
Cairnie Jcn – Elgin (via Buckie)	SC/GNS	6.5.68
Callington – Gunnislake	W/PDSW	7.11.66
Calne – Chippenham	W/GW	20.9.65
Calvert – Ashendon Jcn	LM/GC	5.9.66
Calvert – Claydon	LM/LNE	22.11.65
Cambridge (Chesterton Jcn) – St Ives	E/GE	5.10.70
Cambridge – Bedford St Johns	E/LNW	1.1.68
Cambridge (Shelford) – Sudbury	E/GE	6.3.67
Cardiff (Clarence Rd) – Cardiff General	W/GW	16.3.64
Carlisle (No 3) (via Hawick) – Edinburgh (Portobello East)	SC/NB	6.1.69
Carmarthen – Llandilo	W/LNW	9.9.63
Carmyle – Dumbarton (Douglas Jcn)	SC/CAL	5.10.64
Carmyle – Newton	SC/CAL	5.10.64
Castle Bromwich – Walsall	LM/MID	18.1.65
Castleford Central – Burton Salmon	E/NER	5.1.70
Castleford – Normanton	E/NER	5.1.70
Castleford (Cutsyke Jcn) – Methley North Jcn	E/LY	7.10.68
Chacewater – Newquay	W/GW	4.2.63
Cheadle – Cresswell	LM/NS	17.6.63
Cheltenham Spa – Stratford-on-Avon	W/GW	25.3.68
Cheltenham Spa (St James) – Malvern Road	W/GW	3.1.66
Chester (Northgate) – Mickle Trafford Jcn	LM/CLC	6.10.69
Chester (Northgate) – Hawarden Bridge	LM/GC	9.9.68
Chinley (North Jcn) – Matlock	LM/MID	1.7.68
Chippenham (Thingley Jcn) – Trowbridge	W/GW	6.5.68
Christs Hospital – Guildford	S/LBSC	14.6.65
Christs Hospital (Itchingfield Jcn) – Shoreham	S/LBSC	7.3.66
Church Fenton – Harrogate (Crimple Jcn)	NE/NER	6.1.64
Cirencester Town – Kemble	W/GW	6.4.64
Clevedon – Yatton	W/GW	3.10.66
Coalburn – Hamilton (Haughead Jcn)	SC/CAL	4.10.65
Coatbridge – Rutherglen Jcn	SC/CAL	7.11.66
Colne – Skipton (North Jcn)	LM/MID	2.2.70
Corstorphine – Haymarket (West Jcn)	SC/NB	1.1.68
Cowdenbeath (North Jcn) – Perth (Hilton Jcn)	SC/NB	5.1.70
Cowes – Ryde (St Johns Rd)	S/IWC	21.2.66
Cowlairs Jcn – Springburn	SC/NB	2.3.64
Crianlarich Jcn – Callander	SC/CAL	28.9.65
Crieff – Comrie	SC/CAL	6.7.64
Crieff – Gleneagles	SC/CAL	6.7.64
Cross Gates – Wetherby	NE/NER	6.1.64
Crosshouse – Irvine	SC/GSW	6.4.64
Croxley Green – Bushey & Oxhey	LM/LNW	6.6.66
Cudworth – Monk Spring Jcn	NE/MID	7.9.64
Cymmer Afan – Treherbert	W/RSB	26.2.68
Dalmellington – Ayr (Dalrymple Jcn)	SC/GSW	6.4.64
Dalmeny (North Jcn) – Linlithgow	SC/NB	1.1.73
Dalry (Brownhill Jcn) – Elderslie (Cart Jcn) (via Lochwinnoch)	SC/GSW	27.6.66
Darlington (North Rd) – Barnard Castle (Tees Valley Jcn)	NE/NER	30.11.64
Darvel – Kilmarnock	SC/GSW	6.4.64

Denton – Droylsden	LM/LNW	1.7.68
Denton (Jcn) – Stalybridge (via Hooley Hill)	LM/LNW	1.1.68
Derby – Spondon (Jcn)	LM/MID	7.10.68
Derby (Friargate) – New Basford (Bagthorpe Jcn)	LM/GN	7.9.64
Dereham – Kings Lynn	E/GE	9.9.68
Dereham – Wells-next-the-Sea	E/GE	5.10.64
Dereham – Wymondham	E/GE	6.10.69
Didsbury – Romiley Jcn	LM/CLC/MID	2.1.67
Diggle – Stalybridge (via Micklehurst)	LM/LNW	7.9.64
Douglas West – Lanark/Muirkirk	SC/CAL	5.10.64
Dowlais (Cae Harris) – Nelson & Llancaiach	W/TBJ	15.6.64
Dudley (Blowers Green) – Old Hill	LM/GW	15.6.64
Dudley Port (Horleyfield Jcn) – Swan Village	LM/GW	15.6.64
Dudley Port (High Level) – Dudley	LM/LNW	6.7.64
Dudley – Walsall (Pleck Jcn)	LM/LNW	6.7.64
Dulverton – Barnstaple/Taunton	W/GW	3.10.66
Dulverton – Exeter (Stoke Canon)	W/GW	7.10.63
Dumfries – Dunragit (Challoch Jcn)	SC/GSW/PPW	14.6.65
Dundee (Wormit Jcn) – Newport-on-Tay (East)	SC/NBR	5.5.69
Dundee West – Buckingham Jcn	SC/CAL	3.5.65
Dunfermline (Touch South Jcn) – Stirling (Alloa Jcn)	SC/NBR	7.10.68
Dunstable – Hatfield	LM/GN	26.4.65
Durham (Dearness Jcn) – Bishop Auckland	NE/NER	4.5.64
Durham (Newton Hall Jcn) – Sunderland	NE/NER	4.5.64
East Boldon – Tyne Dock	NE/NER	14.6.65
East Grinstead – Groombridge	S/LBSC	2.1.67
East Grinstead – Three Bridges	S/LBSC	2.1.67
Eastleigh – Romsey	S/LSW	5.5.69
Eccles (Jcn) – Newton-le-Willows (via Tyldesley)	LM/LNW	5.5.69
Edinburgh (Abbeyhill Jcn) – Portobello (via Abbeyhill)	SC/NB	7.9.64
Edinburgh (Princes St) – Slateford Jcn	SC/CAL	6.9.65
Elgin – Cairnie Jcn (via Buckie)	SC/GNS	6.5.63
Elgin – Keith Jcn (via Craigellachie)	SC/GNS	6.5.68
Eridge (Redgate Mill Jcn) – Hailsham	S/LBSC	14.6.65
Etruria – Mow Cop & Scholar Green (Kidsgrove Jcn)	LM/NS	2.3.64
Evercreech Jcn – Highbridge	W/SDJ	7.3.66
Exmouth – Sidmouth Jcn	W/LSW	6.3.67
Fairlie Pier – Fairlie High	SC/GSW	1.10.71
Fawley – Totton	S/SR	14.2.66
Filton Jcn – St Andrews Road	W/GW	23.11.64
Firsby (Bellwater Jcn) – Lincoln Central	E/GN	5.10.70
Firsby (South Jcn) – Grimsby Town	E/GN	5.10.70
Fleetwood – Wyre Dock	LM/PWY	18.4.66
Fordham – Newmarket	E/GE	13.9.65
Fowey – Lostwithiel	W/GW	4.1.65
Fraserburgh – Dyce Jcn	SC/GNS	4.10.65
Fraserburhg – St Combs	SC/GNS	3.5.65
Frodsham – Runcorn	LM/LNW	6.10.75
Gateacre – Hunts Cross Jcn	LM/CLC	17.4.72
Glasgow (Buchanan St) – Sighthill (East Jcn)	SC/CAL	7.11.66
Glasgow (Gorbals) – Strathbungo Jcn	SC/GSW	18.4.66
Glasgow (St Enoch) – Ibrox (Shields Jcn)	SC/GSW	27.6.66
Glazebrook (East Jcn) – Stockport (Tiviot Dale)	LM/CLC	30.11.64
Goole (Oakhill Jcn) – Selby (Barlby Jcn)	NE/NER	15.6.64
Goxhill – Immingham Dock	E/GC	17.6.63
Grange Court – Hereford (Rotherwas Jcn)	W/GW	2.11.64

Grangemouth – Falkirk (Grahamston)	SC/CAL	29.1.68
Grantham (Honington) – Lincoln (Sincil Jcn)	E/GN	1.11.65
Greetland Jcn – Sowerby Bridge	E/LY	5.1.70
Grimsby Town – Firsby (South Jcn)	E/GN	5.10.70
Groombridge – Three Bridges	S/LBSC	2.1.67
Grosmont – Malton (Rillington)	NE/NER	8.3.65
(Grosmont – Pickering reopened 22.4.73 by NYMR)		
Guildford (Peasmarsh Jnc) – Christs Hospital	S/LBSC	14.6.65
Guisborough – Nunthorpe	NE/NER	2.3.64
Guthrie – Forfar	SC/CAL	4.9.67
Hadfield – Penistone	LM/GC	5.1.70
Halwill Jcn – Torrington	W/SR	1.3.65
Halwill Jcn – Bude	W/LSW	3.10.66
Halwill Jcn – Okehampton (Meldon Jcn)	W/LSW	3.10.66
Halwill Jcn – Wadebridge	W/LSW	3.10.66
Hamworthy Jcn – Brockenhurst (via Ringwood)	S/LSW	4.5.64
Harrogate (Dragon Jcn) – Northallerton	NE/NER	6.3.67
Harrow & Wealdstone – Belmont	LM/LNW	5.10.64
Hartlebury – Bewdley	LM/GW	5.1.70
Hartley – Monkseaton	NE/NER	2.11.64
Hartley – Backworth	NE/NER	2.11.64
Hatfield – Dunstable	E/GN	26.4.65
Hayfield – New Mills Jcn	LM/GC & MID	5.1.70
Hayling Island – Havant	S/LBSC	4.11.63
Heads of Ayr – Ayr	SC/GSW	16.9.68
Heath Jcn – Staveley Central (via Chesterfield)	E/GC	4.3.63
Hemyock – Tiverton Jcn	W/GW	9.9.63
Henwick (Leominster Jcn) – Bromyard	W/GW	7.9.64
Hereford – Grange Court	W/GW	2.11.64
Heysham – Morecombe	LM/MID	6.10.75
Highbridge – Evercreech Jcn	W/SDJ	7.3.66
Highgate Road Jcn – Kentish Town Jcn	LM/MID	19.1.64
High Wycombe – Bourne End	W/GW	4.5.70
Hindley – Pemberton	LM/LY	14.7.69
Holt Jcn – Chippenham	W/GW	6.5.68
Holt Jcn – Patney & Chirton	W/GW	18.4.66
Honeybourne (North Jcn) – Cheltenham Spa	W/GW	25.3.68
Honeybourne – Stratford-upon-Avon	W/GW	5.5.69
Hornsea Town – Hull	NE/NER	19.10.64
Horsted Keynes – Haywards Heath	S/LBSC	28.10,63
Horwich – Blackrod	LM/LY	27.9.65
Hough Green – Sankey (via Widnes Ctl)	LM/GC & MID	2.11.64
Huddersfield (Spen Valley Jcn) – Leeds City (Farnley Jcn)	NE/LNW	2.8.65
Hunstanton – Kings Lynn	E/GE	5.5.69
Ilfracombe – Barnstaple Jcn	W/LSW	5.10.70
Ilkley – Skipton	NE/MID	22.3.65
Immingham Dock – Goxhill	E/GC	17.6.63
Immingham Dock – Ulceby	E/GC	6.10.69
Irvine – Crosshouse	SC/GSW	6.4.64
Keswick – Workington (Derwent Jcn)	LM/CKP/LNW	18.4.66
Kettering (Glendon South Jcn) – Nottingham Midland	LM/MID	1.5.67
Killin – Killin Jcn	SC/CAL	28.9.65
Kilmarnock (Hurlford Jcn) – Darvel	SC/GSW	6.4.64
Kilmarnock – Troon (Barassie)	SC/GSW	3.3.69
Kilnhurst (Central) – Sheffield	E/GC	4.9.67
Kingsbridge – Brent	W/GW	16.9.63

Kings Lynn – Dereham	E/GE	9.9.68
Kirkby-in-Ashfield – Radford/Worksop	LM/MID	12.10.64
Kirkcudbright – Castle Douglas	SC/GSW	3.5.65
Kirkintilloch – Lenzie	SC/NB	7.9.64
Laisterdyke – Ardsley (via Morley Top)	NE/GN	4.7.66
Laisterdyke (Adwalton Jcn) – Wakefield Westgate (via Batley)	NE/GN	7.9.64
Laisterdyke (West Jcn) – Bowling Jcn	E/GN	9.6.69
Lanark Jcn – Carstairs (Lanark Jcn)	SC/CAL	18.4.66
Lanark (Smyllum West Jcn) – Muirkirk	SC/CAL	5.10.64
Lancaster (Castle – Lancaster (Green Ayre)	LM/MID	3.1.66
Langholm – Riddings Jcn	SC/NB	15.6.64
Laurencekirk (Kinnaber Jcn) – Perth (Stanley Jcn)	SC/CAL	4.9.67
Leamington Spa (Ave) – Nuneaton (TV)	LM/LNW	18.1.65
Leek – Uttoxeter	LM/NS	4.1.65
Leicester (London Road) – Burton-on-Trent	LM/MID	7.9.64
Leuchars Jcn – St Andrews	SC/NB	6.1.69
Leven – St Andrews	SC/NB	6.9.65
Leven – Thornton Jcn	SC/NB	6.10.69
Lewes – Uckfield	S/LBSC	24.2.69
Liverpool Hunts Cross – Gateacre	LM/CLC	17.4.72
Liverpool (Riverside) – Edge Hill	MDH/LNW	1.3.71
Llanfyllin – Llanymynech	LM/CAM	18.1.65
Long Melford – Sudbury	E/GE	6.3.67
Longport (Jcn) – Tunstall Jcn	LM/NS	27.1.64
Lossiemouth – Elgin (Lossie Jcn)	SC/GNS	6.4.64
Lostwithiel – Fowey	W/GW	4.1.65
Lowestoft (Central) – Yarmouth (South Town)	E/NSJ	4.5.70
Low Moor – Mirfield (via Cleckheaton)	NE/LY	14.6.65
Luffenham – Seaton	LM/LNW	6.6.66
Lyme Regis – Axminster	W/LSW	29.11.65
Mablethorpe – Willoughby	E/GN	5.10.70
Macclesfield – Rose Hill (Marple)	LM/GS & NS	5.1.70
Maerdy – Porth	W/TV	15.6.64
Magdalen Road – March	E/GE	9.9.68
Maldon East – Witham	E/GE	7.9.64
Manchester (Central, Fairfield Jcn) – Chorlton Jcn	LM/GC	5.5.69
Manchester (Central) – Trafford Park	LM/CLC	5.5.69
Manchester (Central) – Chinley	LM/MID/CLC	5.5.69
Mangotsfield – Bath Green Park	W/MID	7.3.66
Manors – Percy	NE/NER	23.7.73
Mansfield (Town) – Radford/Worksop	LM/MID	12.10.64
March – St Ives	E/GE/GN	6.3.67
March – Magdalen Road	E/GE	9.9.68
Market Harborough – Northampton	LM/LNW	26.8.73
Market Harborough – Rugby	LM/LNW	6.6.66
Matlock – Chinley	LM/MID	1.7.68
Melmerby – Harrogate	E/NER	6.3.67
Melmerby – Northallerton (South Jcn)	E/NER	6.3.67
Melton Constable – Sheringham	E/MGN	6.4.64
Mexborough – Barnsley (Quarry Jcn)	E/GC	5.1.70
Mexborough (West Jcn) – Swinton Jcn	E/GC	26.7.65
Middleton-in-Teesdale – Darlington	NE/NER	30.11.64
Millers Dale (Jcn) – Buxton	LM/MID	6.3.67
Millers Dale (Jcn) – Chinley/Matlock	LM/MID	1.7.68
Minehead – Taunton	W/GW	4.1.71
Mirfield (Heaton Lodge Jcn) – Brighouse (Bradley Wood Jcn)	E/LY	5.1.70
Monkseaton – Blyth/Newbiggin	NE/NER	2.11.64

Montgomerie Pier – Stevenston (No 1)	SC/CAL	26.9.67
Morecambe (Prom) – Wennington	LM/MID	3.1.66
Morfa Mawddach (Barmouth Jcn) – Ruabon	LM/GW	18.1.65
Muirkirk – Lanark	SC/CAL	5.10.64
Mussleburgh – Joppa	SC/NB	7.9.64
Nantwich – Wellington	LM/GW	9.9.63
Neasden (via Wembley Stadium) – Neasden	LM/LNE	18.5.68
Neath General – Pontypool Road	W/GW	15.6.64
Nelson (Penallta Jcn) – Ystrad Mynach	W/RHY	15.6.64
Netherfield & Colwick – Nottingham (Victoria)	LM/GN	3.7.67
Newbiggin-by-Sea – Backworth	NE/NER	2.11.64
Newcastle Central – Percy Main (via St Peters)	NE/NER	23.7.73
Newport Pagnell – Wolverton	LM/LNW	7.9.64
Newquay (Tolcarn Jcn) – Chacewater	W/GW	4.2.63
New Romney – Appledore	S/SEC	6.3.67
Neyland – Johnston	W/GW	15.6.64
Normanton (Altofts Jcn) – Castleford (Whitwood Jcn)	E/NER	5.1.70
Northampton (Castle) – Peterborough	LM/LNW	4.5.64
North Walsham – Mundesley-on-Sea	E/NSJ	5.10.64
Nottingham (Radford) – Worksop	LM/MID	12.10.64
Nuneaton (Trent Valley) – Leamington Spa	LM/LNW	18.1.65
Okehampton – Bere Alston	W/LSW	6.5.68
Okehampton (Meldon Jcn) – Wadebridge	W/LSW	3.10.66
Okehampton – Yeoford (Coleford Jcn)	W/LSW	5.6.72
Oswestry – Gobowen	LM/GW	7.11.66
Oswestry – Buttington Jcn	LM/CAM	23.11.64
Oswestry – Whitchurch	LM/CAM	23.11.64
Oxford (North Jcn) – Bletchley	W/LM/LNW	1.1.68
Oxford (Kennington Jcn) – Princes Risborough	W/GW	7.1.63
Padgate Jcn – Sankey (Jcn)	LM/CLC	9.9.63
Padstow – Bodmin Road	W/LSW	30.1.67
Palace Gates (Wood Green) – Seven Sisters	E/GE	7.1.63
Partick West – Dumbarton (Dunglass Jcn)	SC/CAL	5.10.64
Partick West – Possil	SC/CAL	5.10.64
Partick West – Rutherglen	SC/CAL	5.10.64
Patchway (Pilning Jcn) – Severn Beach	W/GW	23.11.64
Pelaw – Durham (via Leamside)	NE/NER	4.5.64
Penistone (Barnsley Jcn) – Barnsley (Exchange)	E/GC	5.1.70
Penistone (Huddersfield Jcn) – Hadfield	E/LM/GC	5.1.70
Penrith – Keswick	LM/CKP	6.3.72
Perth – Cowdenbeath	SC/NB	5.1.70
Perth (Stanley Jcn) – Kinnaber Jcn)	SC/CAL	4.9.67
Peterborough East – Rugby (Midland)	E/LM/LNW	6.6.66
Peterborough (Werrington Jcn) – Boston	E/GN	5.10.70
(Spadling – Peterborough reopened 7.6.71)		
Peterhead – Maud Jcn	SC/GNS	3.5.65
Pilning Jcn – Severn Beach	W/GW	23.11.64
Pinxton (South) – Kimberley (East)	LM/GN	7.1.63
Plymouth (Devonport Jnc) – St Budeaux	W/LSW	7.9.64
Polegate – Hailsham	S/LBSC	9.9.68
Pontefract (Baghill) – Pontefract (Monkhill)	NE/S & K	2.11.64
Pontefract (Monkhill) – Wakefield (Kirkgate)	NE/LYR	2.1.67
Porthcawl – Tondu	W/GW	9.9.63
Portishead – Parson Street	W/GW	7.9.64
Possil – Partick West	SC/CAL	5.10.64
Preston – Southport	LM/LYR	7.9.64

Princes Risborough (Ashendon Jcn) – Calvert	LM/GC	5.9.66
Princes Risborough – Oxford	W/GW	7.1.63
Prudhoe – Scotswood (via North Wylam)	E/NER	11.3.68
Pyle – Portcawl	W/GW	9.9.63
Pyle – Tondu	W/GW	9.9.63
Radford – Worksop	LM/MID	12.10.64
Ramsbottom – Bury	LM/LYR	5.6.72
Renfrew (Wharf) – Hillington (West)	SC/GSW	5.6.67
Richmond (Yorks) – Darlington (Eryholme Jcn)	E/NER	3.3.69
Rochdale (Castleton North Jcn) – Bolton (East Jcn)	LM/LYR	5.10.70
Rose Hill (Marple) – Macclesfield	LM/GC/NS	5.1.70
Royton – Royton (Jcn)	LM/LYR	18.4.66
Rugby – Peterborough (East)	LM/LNW	6.6.66
Rugeley (Trent Valley) – Walsall (Ryecroft Jcn)	LM/LNW	18.1.65
Rutherglen – Dumbarton (Dunglass Jcn)	SC/CAL	5.10.64
Ryde (St Johns Road) – Cowes	S/IWC	21.2.66
(Haven St – Wooton now part of IWR)		
St Boswells – Carlisle	SC/NBR	6.1.69
St Boswells – Edinburgh	SC/NBR	6.1.69
St Boswells – Tweedmouth	SC/NBR/NE	15.6.64
St Combs – Fraserburgh	SC/GNS	3.5.65
St Ives – March (South Jcn)	E/GN/GE	6.3.67
Salisbury (Alderbury Jcn) – West Moors	S/LSW	4.5.64
Scarborough – Whitby	NE/NER	8.3.65
Scotswood (Jcn) – Prudhoe (West Wylam Jcn) (via Newburn)	E/NER	11.3.68
Seaton – Luffenham	LM/LNW	6.6.66
Seaton – Seaton Jcn	WR/LSW	7.3.66
Sengenydd – Aber Jcn Halt	W/RHY	15.6.64
Sharpness – Berkeley Road	W/GW/MID	2.11.64
Shelford – Sudbury	E/GE	6.3.67
Shirebrook Jcn – Warsop Jcn	E/GC	7.9.64
Sidmouth – Sidmouth Jcn	W/LSW	6.3.67
Silloth – Carlisle	LM/NBR	7.9.64
Silverdale – Stoke-on-Trent	LM/NSR	2.3.64
Skipton – Ilkley	NE/MID	22.3.65
Skipton – Colne	LM/MID	2.2.70
Southampton Terminus – St Denys	S/LSW	5.9.66
Sowerby Bridge (Milner Royd Jcn) – Greetland	E/LY	5.1.70
Stafford – Wellington	LM/LNW	7.9.64
Staines West – West Drayton	W/GW	29.3.65
Stonehouse – Strathaven	SC/GSW	4.10.65
Stranraer (Challock Jcn) – Dumfries	SC/PW/GSW	14.6.65
Strathaven – Hamilton (Haughead Jcn)	SC/CAL	4.10.65
Sudbury – Shelford	E/GE	6.3.67
Sunderland – Leamside	NE/NER	4.5.64
Swaffham – Thetford (Roudham Jcn)	E/GE	15.6.64
Swaffham – Dereham	E/GE	9.9.68
Swanage – Wareham (Worget Jcn)	S/LSW	3.1.72
Swansea (Victoria) – Pontardulais	W/LNW	15.6.64
Swinton – Pendleton (via fast lines)	LM/LY	6.9.65
Taunton – Yeovil Pen Mill	W/GW	15.6.64
Tetbury – Kemble	W/GW	6.4.64
Tiverton – Tiverton Jcn	W/GW	5.10.64
Tiverton – Dulverton	W/GW	7.10.63
Todmorden (East Jcn) – Stansfield Hall	LM/LY	1.11.65
Torrington – Barnstaple Jcn	W/LSW	4.10.65

Torrington – Halwill	W/SR	1.3.65
Tyne Commission Quay – Percy Main	E/PTA	4.5.70
Ulceby – Immingham Dock	E/GC	6.10.69
Uttoxeter – Rocester	LM/NSR	4.1.65
Ventnor – Shanklin	S/IWR	18.4.66
Wadebridge – Padstow	W/LSW	30.1.67
Wakefield (Westgate) – Laisterdyke (via Batley)	NE/GNR	7.9.64
Walsall – Castle Bromwich	LM/MID	18.1.65
Walsall (Pleck Jcn) – Wolverhampton (High Level)	LM/LNW	18.1.65
Walsall (Ryecroft Jcn) – Wichnor Jcn	LM/LNW	18.1.65
Walsall (Ryecroft Jcn) – Rugeley (Trent Valley)	LM/LNW	18.1.65
Warrington (Padgate Jcn) – Sankey Jcn	LM/CLC	3.7.67
Wellington (Market Drayton Jcn) – Nantwich	LM/GW	9.9.63
Wellington (Stafford Jcn) – Stafford	LM/LNW	7.9.64
Wells-next-the-sea – Dereham	E/GE	5.10.64
Welshpool (Buttington Jcn) – Whitchurch	LM/CAM	18.1.65
Wembley Stadium Loop – Neasden	LM/LNE	18.5.68
West Moors – Salisbury	S/LSW	4.5.64
Whitby – Scarborough	NE/NER	8.3.65
Wigan (Central) – Glazebrook	LM/GC	2.11.64
Wigan Wallgate (Hindley North) – Pemberton Jcn	LM/LYR	14.7.69
Witham – Yatton	W/GW	9.9.63
Withernsea – Hull (West Parade Jcn)	NE/NER	19.10.64
Wolverhampton (Low Level) – Birmingham (Snow Hill)	LM/GW	6.3.72
Workington – Keswick	LM/CKP/LNW	18.4.66
Wymondham – Dereham	E/GE	6.10.69
Wyre Dock – Poulton-le-Fylde	LM/PWJ	1.6.70
Yarmouth (South Town) – Lowestoft Central	E/NSJ	4.5.70
Yate (South Jcn) – Bristol (Temple Meads)	W/MID	29.12.69
Yatton – Witham	W/GW	9.9.63
Yeovil (Pen Mill) – Yeovil Jcn	W/GW/LSW	6.5.68
Yeovil (Pen Mill) – Yeovil (Town)	W/GW	29.11.65

Bibliography

G. Daniels & L. Dench *Passengers No More* (Ian Allan, 1973)
H.A. Vallance *British Branch Lines* (Batsford, 1965)
D.S. Barrie & C.R. Clinker *The Somerset & Dorset Railway* (Oakwood Press, 1959)
Edward Griffith *The Bishops Castle Railway* (Herald Press, 1969)
Eric S. Tonks *The Shropshire & Montgomeryshire Railway* (Tonks, 1949)
J.I.C. Boyd *The Isle of Man Railway* (Oakwood Press, 1962)
N.J. Stapleton *The Kelvedon and Tollesbury Light Railway* (Forge, 1975)

The author and publisher would like to acknowledge the help and photographs provided by Lens of Sutton, especially the dust jacket and illustrations 4, 9-11, 24-5, 30-1, 61-3, 66, 68-9, 72, 74, 82-4, 90 and 92.